THE
CHRISTMAS
ANGEL

by

Joan Gale Thomas

MOREHOUSE PUBLISHING

© Joan Gale Thomas, 1961 & 1978

First published in Great Britain by
A.R. Mowbray & Co., Ltd.

First American edition published by
Morehouse Publishing
P.O. Box 1321
Harrisburg, PA 17105

ISBN: 0-8192-1724-7
A catalog record for this book is available from
the Library of Congress

Printed in Malaysia

FOR
JEREMY
ROBIN
AND
RICHARD

The Christmas Angel smoothed his wings,
and on his snow white gown
he tied a silver ribbon
with ends that fluttered down.

He took a spray of holly
with berries bright and red,
"For holly tells of Christmas time,"
the Christmas Angel said.

He lit a candle from a star
and then set off abroad
to see if all was ready
for the birthday of his Lord.

He heard the steeple clock strike twelve
below him in the town,
and when the lights had all gone out
the Angel fluttered down.

He landed on a garden gate
then, quiet as a mouse,
he tiptoed up the garden path
towards the sleeping house.

A robin rustled in its nest
high up beneath the eaves;
the Christmas Angel peeped at it
between the ivy leaves.

"I wish you joy," the Angel said,
"and crumbs on Christmas Day;"
he touched the robin's scarlet breast,
then fluttered on his way.

In through an open window
he flew without a sound,
and no one heard, and no one stirred
as the Angel looked around.

He saw the little Christmas tree
the parents had just dressed;
with tinsel, stars, and tiny toys,
all in its Christmas best.

He saw the little gifts that hung
from the branches overhead.
"Each gift to show they truly know
that Christ was born," he said.

"They've thought of gifts for everyone,
I'll leave a gift from me."
And he put his star-lit candle
on top of the Christmas tree.

The little dog was sleeping
in his basket near the stair;
the Angel tiptoed through the hall
and saw him lying there.

He growled a little in his sleep
but, "Hush!" the Angel said.
The little dog looked up at him
and wagged his tail instead.

Then up the stairs the Angel crept
to where the children lay,
fast asleep in bed at last
and dreaming of Christmas Day.

He saw their stockings hanging
at the bottom of each bed.
"I'll just make sure that Santa Claus
remembered them," he said.

He peeped inside and saw that each
was full of pretty things.
The Christmas Angel laughed aloud
and fluttered with his wings.

He played awhile with the nice new toys,
crawling about the floor,
then carefully he put them back
just as they'd been before.

(He knew the children wouldn't mind,
for he was as small as they,
and a busy Christmas Angel
had so little time to play.)

"I wish you a Happy Christmas,"
he whispered to each child—
they never woke when the Angel spoke,
but slightly stirred and smiled—

"Remember who was born today
and thank Him in your prayers..."
he tucked them up, then crept away
and tiptoed down the stairs.

The granny in her room alone
was dreaming of long ago,
when she herself was a little child
and playing in the snow.

The Christmas Angel crept inside
and saw her sleeping there.
He gently kissed her wrinkled cheek
and stroked her silver hair.

He saw the table by the bed
where carefully she'd laid
the little toys and Christmas gifts
that she herself had made.

Wrapping paper, labels too—
she'd thought of everything—
but all she had to tie them with
was a ball of plain brown string.

"But string for things so pretty?"
the Christmas Angel said...
he took his silver ribbon off
and left it there instead.

Then down he flew, and out he flew
into the porch below,
and as he paused upon the step
the cock began to crow.

The stars were pale above his head,
already it was dawn.
"It's Christmas Day," the Angel said,
"the day my Lord was born.

"God bless this house, may all within
remember Him today.
May peace, and love, and kindliness
come down on earth to stay."

He spread his wings to fly away,
then thought of one thing more—
he made a wreath of his holly spray
and hung it on the door.